MENTES LIBRES

INVEST WISELY

 INVEST WISELY

INVEST WISELY

BEGINNER'S GUIDE

INVEST WISELY

INVEST WISELY

INDEX

Introduction

Chapter 1: The Basics

Chapter 2: Should I invest?

Chapter 3: Things... Stabilize

Chapter 4: Making Extra Assets

Chapter 5: Strategy and Style

Conclusion

 INVEST WISELY

Introduction

When it comes to investing, many first-time investors want to get in with both feet. Unfortunately, very few of these investors are successful. Investing in anything requires a certain degree of skill. It is important to remember that few investments are a sure thing - there is a risk of losing your money!

Chapter 1: The Basics

Before taking action, it is best not only to find out more about the investment and how it all works, but also to determine what your goals are.

What do you hope to accomplish with your investments? Will you finance a college education? Buy a home? Retire? Before you invest a single penny, really consider what you hope to accomplish with that investment. Knowing what your goal is will help you make smarter investment decisions along the way!

 INVEST WISELY

The Starting Point

All too often, people invest cash with the dream of getting rich overnight. This is possible, but also rare. It's often a very bad idea to start investing in the hope of getting rich overnight. It's safer to invest the money in such a way that it grows slowly over time, and that it's used for retirement or a young person's education. However, when your investment goal is to become rich quickly, you should learn as much about high-yield, short-term investments as possible before you invest.

You should seriously consider talking to a financial planner before making any investments. Your financial planner can help you determine what kind of investment you should make to achieve your financial goals.

 INVEST WISELY

He or she can give you realistic information about the kind of return you can expect and the time it will take you to reach your particular goals.

Again, remember that investing requires more than calling a stockbroker and telling him or her that you want to buy stocks or bonds. You need a certain amount of research and knowledge about the market when you expect to invest successfully.

 INVEST WISELY

Chapter 2: Should I invest?

Investing has become increasingly crucial over the years, as the future of social security benefits is unknown.

Important information

People want to secure their future and know that if they depend on Social Security benefits, and in some cases retirement plans, they may have a rude awakening when they no longer have the ability to earn a steady income. Investing is the answer to the unknowns of the future.

INVEST WISELY

You may have been saving money in a low-interest savings account over the years. Now, you want to see that money grow at a faster rate.

Maybe you've inherited money or earned some other kind of windfall, and you need a way to make that money grow. Again, investing is the answer.

Investing is also a way to get the things you want, like a new house, a college education for your kids, or expensive "toys. Naturally, your financial goals will determine the type of investment you make.

If you want or need to make a lot of money quickly, you'll be more interested in a higher-risk investment, which will give you a higher

 INVEST WISELY

return in less time. If you're saving for something in the distant future, such as retirement, you'll want to make safer investments that grow over a longer period of time.

The overall purpose of investing is to create wealth and security, over a period of time. It's crucial to remember that you won't always be able to earn an income-you'll eventually want to retire.

Nor can you count on the social security system to do what you expect it to do, nor can you necessarily rely on your company's retirement plan. So, once again, investing is the key to securing your own financial future, but you must make brilliant investments!

 INVEST WISELY

Chapter 3: Things... Stabilize

Before considering investing in any type of market, you should carefully examine your current situation. Investing in the future is a great thing; however, clarifying what is wrong - or possibly wrong - about situations in the present is more crucial.

Get it under control. Get the credit report out. You should do this once a year. It's crucial to know what's on your report, and to clear up any negative items on your credit report as soon as possible. If you have set aside $25,000 to invest, but still have $25,000 of bad credit, you better clean up the credit first!

 INVEST WISELY

Then look at what you are paying each month, and get rid of the expenses that are not necessary. For example, high interest credit cards are not necessary. Pay them off and get rid of them. If you have outstanding loans with high interest rates, pay them too.

If there is nothing else, swap the high interest credit card for a low interest card and refinance the high interest loans with low interest loans. You may have to use some of your investment funds to deal with these issues, however in the long run; you'll find this is the wisest course.

Get in great financial shape - and then improve your financial status with smart investments.

 INVEST WISELY

It doesn't make sense to start investing funds if your bank balance is always low or if you're struggling to pay your monthly bills.

Your investment capital will be better spent to rectify the adverse financial problems that affect you every day.

While you are in the process of getting over your current financial situation, insist on learning about the different types of investments.

That way, when you are in a smart financial state, you will be armed with the knowledge you need to make equally smart investments in your future.

 INVEST WISELY

Chapter 4: Making Extra Assets

Many books and educational plans have been written on how to buy goods wisely. For many people, buying goods is the most beneficial plan for them. But if you have aspirations to acquire assets in order to eventually invest, the question is "Are you willing to produce your assets rather than buy someone else's assets?

Build it up

This book is about passive income and how to take a thought and turn it into an asset that

INVEST WISELY

will develop additional assets. It is not only about how to get a lot of income, but also how to maintain the income that the assets provide and make them produce even more assets in addition to the investment. It reveals how many of the wealthy individuals came to earn the most income.

So if this intrigues you, then please continue. The puzzle is, "How do you produce an asset without spending income to get it?"

"There are people who buy goods and there are people who produce goods."

Many individuals have ideas that can make them rich beyond their wildest aspirations. The point is that most individuals have never been instructed on how to place a business

 INVEST WISELY

structure within their ideas and therefore many of their ideas never take shape or stand on their own.

If you want to be among the people who have extra money to invest, you will have to understand how to establish a business structure within your creative ideas. Once you first try to turn your ideas into a personal fortune, many individuals will say, "You can't do that.

Always remember that nothing erases your incredible ideas more than individuals with few ideas and restricted imagination. The obstacle to turning our ideas into $1, 000000 or even $100,000,000,

The dollar asset is often the struggle between

 INVEST WISELY

our own spirits and our own, often average, brains.

You have to be firm in spirit and firm in your convictions to turn your thoughts into fortunes. Even if you understand the procedure by which your ideas can make you rich, always remember that impressive ideas only become great fortunes if the individual behind the idea is equally willing to be impressive.

It is often difficult to maintain if everyone around you says, "You can't make it. You have to be a very solid spirit to withstand the doubt of those around you. But your spirit must be even less attackable if you are the individual who says to himself, "You can't do that. This doesn't mean that you go blind by not listening to the big, bad ideas of your

 INVEST WISELY

friends or yourself.

Their ideas and input should be heard and often used if their ideas are better than yours. But right now, I'm not talking about simple ideas or advice.

What I am talking about is more than just ideas. I am talking about your emotional state and the willingness to move forward even if you are busy with doubt and outside of the big ideas. No one can tell you what you can or cannot achieve in your life.

Only you are capable of regulating it. Your own greatness is often at the end of the road, and once you try to turn your thoughts into income, there are many times when you reach the end of the road.

 INVEST WISELY

The end of the road is if you are without thoughts, without income, and full of doubt.

If you are able to discover in yourself the spirit to continue, you will discover what it really takes to turn your ideas into incredible assets.

Turning a thought into a great fortune is more a matter of human spirit than the power of the human brain. At the end of each path, the person discovers his or her spirit.

Discovering your spirit and making it solid is more crucial than the idea or business you are formulating. Once you discover your entrepreneurial spirit, you can always take

 INVEST WISELY

really average ideas and turn them into exaggerated fortunes and have money to invest. Always remember that the world is full of individuals with incredible ideas and very few individuals with large fortunes.

 INVEST WISELY

Chapter 5: Strategy and Style

Because investing is not a sure thing in most cases, it is very much like a game - you don't know the outcome until the game has been played and a winner has been declared.

Every time you play almost any kind of game, you have a plan.

Investing is no different - an investment plan is required.

Knowing your tolerance for risk and your

 INVEST WISELY

investment style will help you choose investments more wisely. While there are many different types of investments one can make, there are really only 3 specific investment trends - and those 3 trends relate to your tolerance for risk.

The 3 investment trends are conservative, moderate, and aggressive.

What you need to understand

An investment plan is basically a plan to invest your money in various types of investments that will help you meet your financial goals over a period of time. Each type of investment contains individual investments from which you must select. A clothing store sells clothing - but that clothing

 INVEST WISELY

consists of shirts, pants, dresses, skirts, underwear, etc. The stock market is one type of investment, but it contains several types of stocks, which contain different companies in which you can invest.

If you haven't done your research, it can be very confusing, simply because there are so many different types of investments and individual investments to choose from. This is where your plan comes in, combined with your tolerance for risk and investment tendency.

If you're new to investing, work closely with a financial planner before making any investments. They will help you develop an investment plan that will not only be within the limits of your risk tolerance and investment trend, but will also help you

 INVEST WISELY

achieve your financial goals.

Never invest cash without having a goal and a plan to reach that goal! This is essential. No one gives their money to anyone without knowing what that money is being used for and when they will get it back! If you don't have a goal, a plan, or a scheme, that's essentially what you're doing! Always start with a goal and a plan to reach that goal!

Naturally, if you find that you have a low tolerance for risk, your investment trend will probably be conservative or moderate at best.

If you have a high tolerance for risk, you are likely to be a moderate or aggressive investor. At the same time, your financial goals will also determine the investment

 INVEST WISELY

trend you use.

If you're saving for retirement in your twenties, you should use a conservative or moderate investment trend, but if you're trying to raise the funds to buy a home in the next year or two, you'll want to use an aggressive trend.

Conservative investors want to keep their initial investment. In other words, if they invest $5,000, they want to be sure they'll get their initial $5,000 back. This type of investor commonly invests in stocks and bonds and short-term money market accounts.

A savings account that earns interest is very common for conservative investors.

 INVEST WISELY

A moderate investor commonly invests like a conservative investor, but will use a portion of his or her investment funds for higher risk investments. Many moderate investors invest 50% of their mutual funds in safe or conservative investments, and invest the rest in higher risk investments.

An aggressive investor is willing to take risks that other investors will not. They invest larger amounts of money in higher risk companies in the hope of achieving greater returns, either over time or in the short term. Aggressive investors usually have all or most of their investment funds tied up in the stock market.

Again, the determination of which

 INVEST WISELY

investment trend you will use will be determined by your financial objectives and your tolerance for risk. However, no matter what type of investment you make, you should investigate that investment carefully. Never invest without having all the facts!

 INVEST WISELY

Conclusion

Along the way, you may make some investment mistakes, but there are huge mistakes that you absolutely must avoid if you want to be a successful investor. For example, the biggest investment mistake you might make is not to invest at all, or to stop investing for later. Make your money work for you, even if all you have left is $20 a week to invest!

While not investing at all or procrastinating are huge mistakes, investing before you're in the financial position to do so is another big mistake. Get your current financial situation in order first, and then start investing. Get your credit, pay off high interest loans and

INVEST WISELY

credit cards, and save at least 3 months of living expenses. Once you've done that, you're ready to start letting your money work for you.

Don't invest to get rich quick. It's the riskiest kind of investment there is, and you're more than likely to lose. If it were simple, everyone would do it! Rather, invest for the long term, and have the patience to weather the storms and let your money grow. Only invest in the short term when you know you'll need the money soon, and then move on to secure investments, such as certificates of deposit.

Don't put all your eggs in one basket. Spread them out into different types of investments to get the best returns. In the same way, don't move your money around too much. Let it run. Choose your investments carefully,

 INVEST WISELY

invest your money and let it grow. Don't panic if the stock drops a few dollars. If the stock is stable, it will rise again.

Remember, no risk, no gain, but be smart!

 INVEST WISELY

Visit our author page on Amazon and get more **MENTES LIBRES!**

http://amazon.com/author/menteslibres

If you wish, you can leave a comment on this book by clicking on the following link so that we can continue to grow! Thank you very much for your purchase!

https://www.amazon.com/dp/B084F374GX

www.ingramcontent.com/pod-product-compliance
Lightning Source LLC
Chambersburg PA
CBHW050307220526
45465CB00002B/861